After Our War

JOHN BALABAN

After Our War

UNIVERSITY OF PITTSBURGH PRESS

Feffer and Simons, Inc., London
Manufactured in the United States of America

Library of Congress Cataloging in Publication Data

Balaban, John, birth date
  After our war.
  (Pitt poetry series)
  I. Title.
PS3552.A44A7   813'.5'4   73-13313
ISBN 0-8229-5247-5

Some of the poems in this book appeared earlier in *The American Scholar,
Approach, Chelsea 24/25* ("Mau Than"), *Eating the Menu* (Prentice-Hall, 1974),
Friends Journal, Modern Poetry in Translation, no. 17, the *New York Times,
Prairie Schooner,* and *The Western Humanities Review.* They are reprinted here
with the permission of the editors.

    In addition, we gratefully acknowledge the permission of the Pennsylvania
State University Press to reprint "In Hyperborea" from *Direction in Literary
Criticism* (1973) and "Don Diego Garcia," "For Miss Tin in Hue," and
"Graveyard at Bald Eagle Ridge" from the October 1972, January 1971, and
April 1971 issues of the *Journal of General Education.*

    International Voluntary Services, Inc., and Roger Montgomery graciously
permitted us to print the prose sections of "The Gardenia in the Moon."

*The publication of this book is supported
by a grant from the National Endowment for the Arts
in Washington, D.C., a Federal agency.*

for Lonnie

Contents

After Our War

Carcanet: After Our War

"For thy Carcanets of Pearle, shalt thou have Carcanets of Spyders,
or the Greene Venomous Flye, Cantharides."
—Thomas Nashe, *Christe's Teares Over Jerusalem*

When we blighted the fields, the harvests replied:
"You have blighted your flesh." Muck-marrowed,
bones ungluing like book paste; nerve hems
shredded or grimed in something foul, leaking,
we visit each other like a plague. Kiss-Kiss.
Intelligence is helplessly evil; words lie.
Morally quits, Hieronymo gnashes off his tongue,
spits out the liver-lump to a front-row lap,
but wishes, then to explain; even: to recite poetry.
Yesterday a pig snouting for truffles uncovered
moles, blind and bellyful of *Paradise Lost*.
Gleeful, let us go somewhere to curse God and die.

To market they came from land and sea, the air:
"A mighty fine place," one General agreed.
They reined in their horses and looked down to find
an old beggar woman sneaking by in their shadows.
"Call in the Doctor," barked the Seal from the Sea.
A Fourth Horseman reined up, brandishing a smile
for half the lady's face was a red hanging bag,
one eye a wart strudel, her chin a grainy sac.
She begged. The Doctor-General proffered a pin,
"My Lady, in our hour of need." He pick-pricked a node.
A yellow milk-water splashed her blouse, spurted
curdles on the Horsemen's boots, streaked to the gutter,
filled up the streets and gushed against doorsills.
The old lady cackled; the four generals beamed,
and summoned a palfrey for Their Lady to ride.
They had found Home, were Active. As they rode off
the hoofs of their horses spattered the walks.

At that the fat bullets started to jump;
some whined to splice the prism of an eye, others
bled the marrow from a rib. Windshields spidered;

the Spiders ran off, eight-legged, fast, with money,
more than you can guess, stuck to the hairy legs.
Spontaneous Generation: the Bore-Flies sang,
"Every wound has two lips, so give us a kiss."
Then a two-headed cow jumped over the moon,
kicked over its lantern. Fire caught Straw.
The cow burst like a 500-lb. bomb. Everyone
came running—all the old folks—Slit Eye
and Spilled Guts, Fried Face and little Missy Stumps.
They plaited a daisy chain. This necklace. For you.

That Man

pissing off the front stoop
into the night, his urine
splattering the crusted snow,
is me. He listens
to his water and to the water
of the brook beyond the alders,
watching the oblate moon careen
above the India-ink hemlocks
and hearing the brook nag: "Time
flows. Flowing times."
Because a girl he's begun to know
is now bathing in the tub,
he's skunked outside. Because
of that because, I've stepped outside.
I should go and introduce them,
if I could. But I too am baffled
by the moon rocking in the hemlocks,
by the moons rickling in the stream.

The Guard at the Binh Thuy Bridge

How still he stands as mists begin to move,
as morning, curling, billows creep across
his cooplike, concrete sentry perched mid-bridge
over mid–muddy river. Stares at bush green banks
which bristle rifles, mortars, men—perhaps.
No convoys shake the timbers. No sound
but water slapping boat sides, bank sides, pilings.
He's slung his carbine barrel down to keep
the boring dry, and two banana-clips instead of one
are taped to make, now, forty rounds instead
of twenty. Droplets bead from stock to sight;
they bulb, then strike his boot. He scrapes his heel,
and sees no box bombs floating towards his bridge.
Anchored in red morning mist a narrow junk
rocks its weight. A woman kneels on deck
staring at lapping water. Wets her face.
Idly the thick Rach Binh Thuy slides by.
He aims. At her. Then drops his aim. Idly.

Pentangle

"Then þay schewed hym þe schelde, þat was of schyr gouleȝ,
Wyth þe pentangel de-paynt of pure golde hweȝ;
& quy þe pentangel apendeȝ to that prince noble,
I am in-tent yow to telle, þof tary hyt me schulde."
—*Sir Gawain and the Green Knight*

1 Augury for a Soul So Dry It Would Fly

While overhead the dry,
dusty, parchment wings
of brown, broad-winged,
white and wide-winged,
dragonflies
rustled and tattered
—dragonflies,
which, incredibly,
were wanting to mate—
the wind picked up,
reminding the sailboats
of the shore and
even my clean white pages
fluttered,
amorous of the wind.

2 A Man Goes Afishing in a Certain Stream

At the end of the yellow pool,
islanded with floating fennel,
where the blue herons fish,
there, beneath the rock ledge,
under the plunging spillway
below its clean harrow's teeth,
brown minnows dart
after a duck's white feather,
and dart after each other
in the rake-toothed spillway
to sputter about the bright shallows
like chitlings in a copper pan.

It is not hard to see
in their finny wriggles
the signatures of human delight;
in the pool, a human place.
For in a rilly world
time is told on bubbles:
foam in the spring,
pale flecks in the fall.
In October, triremes of leaves
choke the harbored heavens
and suffocate the foam strokes.
Come winter, time seals.
One imagines these minnows
like wicks in the candled ice,
the heavens' hard dome of ice.
But now, if one tosses a penny,
it tumbles: brightly; darkly,
and the fish merely make
another arabesque.

3   The Dirae

The oaks are riding the autumn winds.
Beyond their tossing tops
rest the hills you loved,
across the rocky Shenandoah
and the cut-current Potomac
smelly as wet, summer-wild dogs.
In the spare red cedars
and the sparse white spruce
there stir no loud movements,
and gnats whiz sullenly.
Bees hum about the hills' sides,
bobbing the raggedy goldenrod,

Queen Anne's Lace and thistle.
Rasping harshly, a catbird cries
on the towpath. A turtle hisses
under a withered May Apple
At Harper's Ferry where John Brown
blew his mind's arsenal, where
rusting root-ways of twisted gun barrels
mat the grassy floor of the old armory,
there was time once for us to sit
on the gallery and hear the evening
called in by the whippoorwills.
Then, to love's eye, stick-stubs
streamered with grass in the water
were emerald snakes, gliding.
Blue dragonflies seemed needles
grown papery tat-tatter wings.
Time once. But our time will not
circle back with the river valley seasons
where the Shenandoah licks the face
of the Potomac. In the morning
there will be no waking at your side.
Alone but for three sullen, dry-faced
sisters, I rock and creak my chair
on the peeling stoop. I wait to go.
"*Rura valete iterum tuque optima Lydia salve.*"

4   Lo, He Sees Four Men Loose, Walking in the Midst of the Fire

Christians have always been pilgriming;
setting out with clamshell hat and clapper;
begging barefoot and beating their backs.
Hard-seeking fellows, scabbing their skins;
swigging down wormwood, gulping down gall.

Just as soon would they fry on pyres
of martyrdom as bathe in a river of mercy.
Yet, ever since pitch-dipped Christians
lighted Nero's dinner parties, we have
understood the purgation of fire. Fire
shall come to roast up Babylon; fire shall
teach Ezekiel; fire shall light Job's pain.
Nowhere but in the bible of the spirit
could Shadrach, Meshach, and Abednego
crack jokes in Nebuchadnezzar's fiery furnace.
O Lord, I go into a land where napalm
makes men dance a crazy jig; where
Nero sets his sights by human flares.
I ask for clear water, good earth and air.

5   The Dream of the Rood

Whan I see on rode
Jhesu my lemman,
and biside him stonden
Marie and Iohan,
and his rigge i-swongen,
and his side i-stongen
for the love of man:
Wel owe I to wepe,
and synnes forlete,
If *I* of love can,
if I of *love* can,
'if I of love *can.*

A Floating Opera

"Nature is at times a shameless playwright"
—John Barth, *The Floating Opera*

Here where the lava slid into the sea
hissing up steam clouds; burbled into stone,
a moonscape of razor-lace craters, gray flats,
knee-high ridges; pocked colossal boulders.
The tides chafe canyons day and night
scooping out clear, shallow, shadowed wells,
sand-bottomed cisterns, where with sun shaft
and tide froth, plays a certain metaphor.
At the shadow's step, crabs antic out of reach.
In the dark crooks of the tide-wash basin
the ink purple urchins wait for whatever.
Twist the blade to pry one out—the little nettles
would prick your hand—flip it over:
the winking anus-mouth, stuffed with meats.
Blue neon fingerlings flit below a rock.
Foot-finned eels shake off to darker rests.
The hermit, half-inch crabs of ivory claw,
pop-dot blue eyes and strawberry whiskers,
labor off under any dead creature's shell.
A filtering ray spots on a zebra fish
fluttering at the door of his air-bubbled cave.
Startle this catch hole, it contrives barrenness;
light probes a convict's wall; tides rake only sands.
Sunned and mooned, a fishbowl nonetheless
for the plover stropping his scissor-bill,
for the sea punching a hole from below the shelf,
flushing out, baring, a wrinkled socket.
And daily, as tides strake and go,
one hears the tick of the salt clock.
In sea buckets close to the sun, salt
milk films, crystal lattices lock out air.
Instead of wriggle and nip and perky spine:
shells, endoskeletons, sand dollars, snails.
Finally, the white cataracted eye.

Along The Mekong

1   Crossing on the Mekong Ferry,
Reading the August 14 *New Yorker*

Near mud-tide mangrove swamps, under the drilling sun,
the glossy cover, styled green print, struck the eye:
trumpet-burst yellow blossoms, grapevine leaves,
—nasturtiums or pumpkin flowers? They twined
in tangles by our cottage in Pennsylvania.
Inside, another article by Thomas Whiteside.
2, 4, 5-T, teratogenicity in births;
South Vietnam 1/7th defoliated; residue
in rivers, foods, and mother's milk.
With a scientific turn of mind I can understand
that malformations in lab mice may not occur in children
but when, last week, I ushered hare-lipped, tusk-toothed kids
to surgery in Saigon, I wondered, what did they drink
that I have drunk. What dioxin, picloram, arsenic
have knitted in my cells, in my wife now carrying
our first child. Pigs were squealing in a truck.
Through the slats, I saw one lather the foam in its mouth.

2   River Market

Under the tattered umbrellas, piles of live eels
sliding in flat tin pans. Catfish flip for air.
Sunfish, gutted and gilled, cheek plates snipped.
Baskets of ginger roots, ginseng, and garlic cloves;
pails of shallots, chives, green citrons. Rice grain
in pyramids. Pig halves knotted with mushy fat.
Beef haunches hung from fist-size hooks. Sorcerers,
palmists, and, under a tarp: thick incense, candles.
Why, a reporter, or a cook, could write this poem
if he had learned dictation. But what if I said,
simply suggested, that all this blood fleck,

muscle rot, earth root and earth leaf, scraps
of glittery scales, fine white grains, fast talk,
gut grime, crab claws, bright light, sweetest smells
—Said: a human self; a mirror held up before.

3   Waiting for a Boat to Cross Back

Slouched on a bench under some shade,
I overhear that two men shot each other on the street,
and I watch turkey cocks drag cornstalk fans
like mad, rivaling kings in Kabuki
sweeping huge sleeve and brocaded train.
The drab hens huddle, beak to beak,
in queenly boredom of rhetoric and murder.
A mottled cur with a grease-paint grin
laps up fish scales and red, saw-toothed gills
gutted from panfish at the river's edge.

Mother Egret

Translation of a Vietnamese folk lyric

Egrets bear egret sons.
Mother's after shrimp; little one's at home.
Far off has Mother Egret flown
to alight . . . and be roped by Brother Eel!
Nearby's a man in a bamboo keel
sliding through cattails to catch eel and fowl.
Poling clumsily, he rams the prow.
Brother Eel dives down; Mother flies off.

Writes Xenophanes, Before Choosing Exile

I say, what does it matter if the women
of Colophon are no longer given
to go the streets in flowing, sea purple robes?

That the pipe no longer leads seductive odes
sung in the voluptuous Lydian mode?
That the Medes now temper their swords on our hearths?

Walking on Colophon's foggy shore at night,
one is the center of a circle of sight.
The wheel of a chariot has one locus.

The eye circumscribes the radius of the real.
One walks on. The fog cloaks what it revealed.
Before, it opens like the folds of a robe.

Strained with a vision, the self begins to breathe.
On Colophon's shore by the warm, dark sea
cymbals crash. Flutes shrill. Slowly, feet stir the sand.

Orpheus Slaughtered near the River

At morning his head's heat
blew wide its ports.

Clean and lyric wind
circled and cooled

the skull's open grain
before it could take on fears

like a sawed limb does blight.
His ear was a swallow.

Brightest of stones, his eye
danced under clear, sliding water.

Orpheus in the Upper World

By the pasture's chewed and narrow path
he discovered asters lighting
the evening way like lamps,
and there below, tufted thistles
perched on meadow stalks
like sparrows brusking for flight.
Butterflyweeds spread orange wings
brighter than any flutter-by's.
Fanspreads of yarrow, vervain plumes
he saw, and evening primrose, flower of love.

Knowing these, which summers past
he could not name, delighted him.
For when his order had burst his head,
like sillowy seeds of milkweed pod,
he learned to pay much closer watch
to all things, even small things,
as if to discover his errors.

Hissarlik

This is the dust
of nine cities,
royal as the poppy,

each grown
over the sediment
of the last.

Here the dust of Achaeans
and of Priam's sons
mingles

with the sherds and stones,
the bones—remnants
of slaves and lords.

Nine cities,
born in turn
upon the death mounds

of the former,
entombing themselves,
building this hill.

This is the hill
of Hissarlik where
the limbs of countless

entwine and dissolve
under the common earth
which we sift and shovel

into fluted ash cans
that lie empty now
like broken white columns.

Mau Than

A Poem at Tet for To Lai Chanh

1   Friend, the Old Man that was last year
has had his teeth kicked in; in tears
he spat back blood and bone, and died.
Pielike, the moon has carved the skies
a year's worth to the eve. It is Tet
as I sit musing at your doorstep,
as the yellowed leaves scratch and clutter.
The garden you dug and plotted
before they drafted you, is now
stony, dry, and wanting a trowel.
"For my wife," you said, taking a plum,
but the day never came nor will it come
to bring your bride from Saigon.
Still the boats fetch stone, painted eyes on
their prows, plowing the banana-green river;
and neighbor children splash and shiver
where junks wait to unload their rock.
But shutters locked, the door of your house is locked.

2   A year it was of barbarities
each heaped on the other like stones
on a man stoned to death.
One counts the ears on the GI's belt.
Market meats come wrapped in wrappers
displaying Viet Cong disemboweled.
Cries come scattering like shot.
You heard them and I heard them.
The blessed unmaimed may have too.
So many go stumping about.
The night you left I turned off Hoa Binh
and saw a mined jeep, the charred family.
A Vietnamese cop minded the wreckage;
his gold buck teeth were shining

in a smile like a bright brass whistle.
Can you tell me how the Americans,
officers and men, on the night of
the mortaring, in the retching hospital,
could snap flash photos of the girl whose
vagina was gouged out by mortar fragments?
One day we followed in a cortege
of mourners, among the mourners, slowing walking,
hearing the clop of the monk's knocking stick.

3   If there were peace, this river would be
a peaceful place. Here at your door
thoughts arrive like rainwater, dotting,
overspreading a dry, porous rock.
In a feathery drizzle, a man and wife
are fishing the river. The sidling waves
slap at her oar as she ladles the water
and fixes the boat with bored precision.
His taut wrists fling whirring weights;
the flying net swallows a circle of fish.
His ear wears a raindrop like a jewel.
Here at evening one might be as quiet
as the rain blowing faintly off
the eaves of a rice boat sliding home.
Coming to this evening
after a rain, I found a buff bird
perched in the silvery-green branches
of a water-shedding spruce. It was
perched like a peaceful thought. Then
I thought of the Book of Luke and, indeed,
of the nobleman who began a sojourn
to find a kingdom and return.

4 Out of the night, wounded
with the gibberings of dogs,
wheezing with the squeaks of rats,
out of the night, its belly split
by jet whine and mortar blast,
scissored by the claws of children,
street sleepers, ripping their way free
from cocoons of mosquito netting
to flee the rupturing bursts
and the air dancing with razors
—out, I came, to safe haven.
Nor looked, nor asked further.
Who would? What more? I said.
I said: Feed and bathe me.
In Japan I climbed Mt. Hiei in midwinter.
The deer snuffled my mittens.
The monkeys came to beg.
I met Moses meeting God in the clouds.
The cold wind cleared my soul.
The mountain was hidden in mist. Friend,
I am back to gather the blood in a cup.

Graveyard at Bald Eagle Ridge

Solomon's Seal, false and true,
Jewel Weed, and Arrowroot.
Here swallows, snatching at bugs,
skirt the cornstalks' tassled tops
and dart above the sunken stones
of the hillside graveyard.

Farmers hold dearly to their dead:
the dead in childbirth and in war,
dead with sickness, dead with age.
Neatly as a kitchen garden,
they have tended the tombstones.
But, see, a bucktoothed woodchuck
burrows out a daughter's bones.
Will a tooth churn up? Cracked
wishbones of a child's hand?

Rainfogs lift up from the valley
which the dead are set to view.
Cowbells clang in earshot, while
a white nag chomps amid the clover.
Looking out, the dead—the Shirks,
Browns, Gingerys, and Rines—
find their children green-haired,
socket-blind, and lying beside them.
In this year of our Lord, 1969,
a sparse generation tills the land.

Appalachian Train Stop

The winter noon's glare chilled to dusk
as the sun lapsed between two hills

cusping the twilight arc
in a tremolo of blue. The day

closed like a shutting eye.
From a platform bench, two boys in jeans

stared up at foundry smoke
drifting across the legs of Orion.

One picked his boot without a word.
Their soiled grip hid a Colt revolver.

Now, years later, what proofs are there
of smoke trails, train stop, of even the town?

Why, if it is not a clear winter's eve,
one may doubt that Orion hunts the sky.

Having Discovered a Snail Shell, the Poet Presents It in the Metaphysical Manner

My love, take up this little shell
and tell me if you see
inlaid in lacquered locutions
our love's geometry:

The centric chambers wind around
down to the central heart.
Reversed, these spirals spiral out
expanding bands of art.

Its opaque, volute volume
enlarges as it grows.
If love should live forever,
love would all the world enclose.

Blue Morning Coat

It was dawn once more
  like the blue morning coat
When I turned the stile
  with the cigarette-burnt cuff
At Tokyo Customs.
  which you wore that morning
Shifting an old bouquet
  for the hotel room and separation
The kimono-woman ahead
  when the sparrows were chitterelling
Dropped blue petals on the floor
  in the close city air.

The Gardenia in the Moon

For David Lane Gitelson, 1942–1968

1 In Pennsylvania Woods

The wind was husking, hushing, hosting,
worrying the slimed leaves of the wood.
Moon's light, thick as Witches Butter,
stuck to branch bark and to lifting leaves.
Standing under fitful oaks, under Orion
bullying the gods, I saw car lights
stabbing past the rain-blacked trunks,
and heard the Peacock shriek, the Owl,
hoot. Men had landed on the moon.
As men shot dirty films in dirty motel rooms,
guerrillas sucked cold rice and fish.
Wind-spooked leaves scratched my cheek.
Blood on the bark stung the hand.
In a puddle's moon eye I saw a shape:
A machine gun was cracking like slapping sticks.
A yelling man smacked into the smooth canal.

MONTHLY REPORT—AGRICULTURE

DATE   :   October, 1967
STATION   :   Hue-Duc, An-Giang—Region IV
IVS TEAM MEMBER   :   Dave Gitelson

At least two varieties of fruit trees here suffer badly from disease.
Infected custard apple trees, "mang cau ta," produce fruit that's
hard, black and spore-filled. This is a very prevalent disease, so
much so that people are discouraged from planting this tree,
formerly a popular orchard variety. Another disease affects
jackfruit trees, "mit," the fruit first develops brown patches then
turns mushy. I'd appreciate advice on how to deal with these
diseases. Dithane and other fungicides are available in Long-
Xuyen but they're expensive.

Previously I've had talks with the province and MSCR on
possible ways to reduce civilian war casualties, e.g. get the families
of soldiers out of the remote outposts by providing them housing
in more secure areas. Late last month, after one man was killed
and another wounded by air-fire in a free fire zone west of
Vong-The Village, the local people made some suggestions that
might also apply to other areas. First they asked the zone be
suspended, but in lieu of that they said that if the outposts closest
to the zone, which in this case includes a company headquarters,
could have been contacted by radio, the men might not have been
shot, since they were known to several of the local soldiers. The
automatic procedure is for the L-19 pilot to radio the District
for permission to fire, but whether the local units are contacted
is up to the district chief. In this case there may have been reasons
outside of his presence in the free fire zone to suspect the dead
man—and other reasons to suspect the suspicion.

3 A Cyclo Ride to Town

Early evening airs cool the cheek;
the dust is down on the rutted road.
Lurching handlebars as we wheel up,
the cyclo driver hoots and jings his bell
at the dog that lolls panting in our way:
the weary bitch drags off her heavy tits.

From the bouncing carriage, one studies
the old man's dry calves, bulging out
blue ropy veins as tendons stretch and ease.
An axle, a fender, his head bobbles
on a rooster's neck. Teeth gritting dust,
he pedals us past a tin bus decaying
by the roadside: bleached, roofless,
floorboards dropped, the stripped seat frames
jut like knobby vertebrae upon a beach.

We pass the pond links where fishermen,
anonymous as jellyfish tracing a shore,
hurl parabolas to snag the glinting carp,
And hopping home from market, a one-legged girl
pauses to tuck a pant leg to her stump.

Jolting past a dust-caked banana grove,
by the Post Gate we come upon the crowd
gawking at the farmer hauled in like a pig:
riddled dead, blood-splotched, trussed to a pole.
Striking the smooth macadam of a city street,
we roll down the boulevard, past the market
along the river sliding under reeling birds,
past the dry fountain with its sandbagged gun nest
and stop at the French governor's empty mansion,
roofed with orange tiles, walled with chipping stucco.

The gate guard salutes, then grins with history
as an American strides the pebbled walkway
to the garden at the rear of the elegant house,
whose formal paths, boxwoods, flower beds
—laid in a helplessly exact geometry—
have been tank-tracked by the armored unit
bivouacked beneath the high, threshing palms.

The scent of gardenia and campsmoke shifts
through the strung laundries and poncho tents.

4

MONTHLY REPORT—AGRICULTURE

PERIOD   :   December, 1967
STATION   :   An-Giang, Hue Duc—Region IV
IVS TEAM MEMBER :   Dave Gitelson

3 weeks ago Tuesday morning there was an airstrike on the
outskirts of Tan Tay Hamlet, Vong-The Village, which killed
immediately 4 children 2 women and 3 men and wounded 12
others. In two families both parents were killed. Later one of the
wounded, a man, died. A community of 33 families was wiped
off the map. Their homes were mostly destroyed along with their
boats and livestock. The survivors arrived in the market with
nothing but the clothes they were wearing at the time of the
attack, that is with no bedding or food.
I've been told this was an unavoidable accident; the victims were
at fault; and all necessary precautions were taken. I'm not
satisfied that this is true. I have the following facts and questions
in mind.

1) The Vietnamese and American military were jointly respons-
ible for the strike. The planes that did the bombing were Vietnamese Air Force. There was an L-19 in the area with a Vietnamese observer and an American pilot-observor. The District
and Province gave their approval. Their MACV counterparts say
they're just advisors—but none of them advised against the
attack.
MACV claims there were VC in the area dug in and firing
at the planes. All right, the L-19 was up and he ought to know.
But no VC casualties came my way. And it's hard to have total
faith in MACV Intelligence when 24 hours after the attack there
were people at MACV subsector who didn't know the majority of
casualties were women and children and 3 weeks after the attack

30

a senior officer at MACV Long-Xuyen apparently wasn't certain any children had been killed at all.

But what if the area had been swarming with VC. L-19 pilots in Region I have told me they'd never advise a strike if there were civilians in the area. There haven't been any American casualties in Hue-Duc that I know of since I've been here; the pressure doesn't exist like near DaNang and Hue. Why should an airstrike have been called with civilians so close? If those had been American kids on the ground, could such a thing possibly have happened?

The attack came around 11 A.M. MACV claims a marking round was dropped and the civilians given some time to clear the area. How long I can't recall—20 minutes? a half hour? At the least why couldn't the area have been leafletted or otherwise put on warning and the civilians given 2 or 3 hours to get out of the way?

Both the Vietnamese and American military were aware before the attack of the danger of civilian casualties in this area, which has had 3 fishermen—1 dead, 2 wounded—hit by airfire in the past 2 months.

Admittedly at least 2 of these men were hit when they entered the free fire zone 3 kilometers west of the site of the bombing.

2) The Vietnamese authorities in the Village and District point to a bulletin sent by the Village Council in September warning the people in the area of the bombing that it's a dangerous zone and that they should move or the government wouldn't take responsibility for loss of life or property. On the basis of this bulletin the District Chief is refusing to consider paying compensation for property damage, although something may be paid the families of the dead and wounded. And yet it was no secret these people were out there three-quarters of a mile from the headquarters of a PF company. They've been there for years.

They were important suppliers of fish to the village market, and they farm, along with some absentee farmers, more than a thousand hectares of rice in that area. If the government wanted them out of the area, all that was necessary was for the outpost controlling the canal to forbid them passage back from the market. Furthermore the village council regularly issues letters of permission to fish and graze cattle in the area and to travel on the canal during daylight. I've seen at least 10 such permits, newly issued, admittedly not to the people resident in the area but to others, some of whom claim minor damage in the bombing.

3) Perhaps the essence of the matter is that the Vietnamese and American military don't feel any mistake has been made. When I asked a MACV senior officer in Long-Xuyen whether in these circumstances this doesn't make the civilians just so much foliage to shoot through, he agreed. He said the people were lucky, that if the heliocopters had been in proper strafing position, no one would have got out alive.

4) After the attack, little concern was shown for the survivers. Fortunately most of them have relatives in the market willing to help them out. Presumably many of them have no legal means of support outside of these relatives, the two families of orphans at least. At least one family resorted to some house-to-house begging. 4 days after the attack the District and MACV sent 32 bags of rolled oats and 32 cans of cooking oil. This shipment turned over in the canal before it reached the village and MACV subsector was incapable of replacing it or supplementing it. 3 weeks after the attack processing has just started on applications for compensation for the wounded and families of the dead. So to date what the people have from their government and the US authorities is 32 bags of wet oatmeal and 32 cans of oil.

5 Gardenia

The scent of gardenia and campsmoke shifts
across laundries, hammocks, and tents.
With white, thick, waxy, double petals a jasmine
gardenia reeks, a prostitute in the stripped garden.
Under a planked jetty, some soldiers and their little sons
skinny dip, foaming the silted river with suds.
Below a lotus blooming in the mucky shallows,
a crab sidles through a basket rotting in the mud.
In midstream, huge egrets lift off the bamboo marshes.
I hear my name called: "Mr. American!"
by a pajamaed young mother who grins and beckons,
slapping a broken slipper and waddling my way.
Closing to her thumb the fingers of a white hand,
in the bud-hole of those loose doubled petals
she pokes her other index, and smiles. Tilting her chin,
she pokes her finger again and again and smiles.

6

TO   Dan Whitfield   Date: Jan. 30, 1968

FROM   Roger Montgomery

SUBJECT   A Chronology

On Friday evening, Jan. 26, I met the plane coming in from Long
Xuyen, bringing Tom Fox, who was to change planes and go on
to Saigon, after visiting Phil Yang in Long Xuyen. Tom brought
the first word that Dave had been captured and reported killed.
After hearing all of the information that Tom had, I quickly
returned to the CORDS office to call you and relay the small
amount of info that we had. That evening I called Col. Lane in
Long Xuyen, and also Bob Flores called me in Can Tho. The first
reports were that a man who had been called a "taxi driver"
(perhaps of a water taxi boat?) had reported to officials in Hue
Duc district that he had seen Dave captured by four VC and
taken off a distance into a woodsy section and then heard four
shots. That evening there was also a report that somebody in
Hue Duc had seen a body. It was not confirmed by any American
or Vietnamese Government official that it was Dave and there
was no certainty where it was. The next morning I drove to Long
Xuyen with John Balaban. . . .

Col. Lane, who in his briefing to John and me expressed his dis-
like for Dave and related how they had had serious disagreements
(especially concerning the bombing incident reported in Dave's
last monthly report) said that they were making all efforts to
recover his body but that he had been consulting his rule books

34

all morning to find out if the military should handle civilians bodies, and couldn't find a guiding ruling...

Finally around three, it was reported back on the radio that the body had been recovered by the soldiers on the operation, but the MACV people said they could not call the chopper until it had been identified by Americans. The MACV subsector people immediately proceeded by boat to the location where the body was brought to, at the base of Ba The mountain, and two of the MACV fellows identified it as being Dave, one of the men was Spec4 Gerasimo. This made it around 4:30 or 5:00 in the evening. Then a helicopter was finally called through 9th Vietnamese Division, and a request was finally made for complete transportation all the way to Saigon or somewhere where there was a mortuary. After a while, a helicopter finally arrived and went straight to Ba The where the MACV people had also gathered up all of Dave's belongings and brought it in to Long Xuyen. As there was some confusion as to whether this helicopter should take both the body and the belongings straight to Saigon, or to transfer it to a fixed wing airplane at the airport which would then proceed on to Saigon. As everybody, all the CORDS people, including Mr. Elliot was waiting at the heliport, the helicopter circled, and finally landed. It was then learned that approval was not given by G-4 in Can Tho to move the body that evening, and even Mr. Elliot calling CORDS in Can Tho and notifying them that there were no facilities for keeping a body in Long Xuyen, could not get any kind of transportation, Dave's body had already been exposed, and evidently in the water for up to 36. The extra twelve hours of sitting locked up in a room at the Long Xuyen hospital did not at all improve the condition of the body and in fact left little for the mortuary to work with...

35

3

He also was onto something that was extremely sensitive, which he had mentioned to Tom Fox and me just the previous Wednesday (or Thursday) that one day prior to Senator Edward Kennedy's trip to Hue due district to visit the refugees that the refugee chief had come out and told the refugees that if they spoke out complaining to Senator Kennedy about treatment in the refugee camp that he would have them killed or imprisoned or such. Some of the refugees were so hopping mad that after the visit of Senator Kennedy, that they had written a letter complaining to Vice President KY, and Dave had asked them to give him copies of the letter . . . he would have it translated and a copy sent to Senator Kennedy himself. I believe that a copy was not sent to the Senator but that a copy was given to Mr. Chuck Husick of NLD/CORDS in the abscence of Mr. Steve Whilden the CORDS refugee man. It has also been reported to me and this is only hearsay, that Mr. Whilden's interpreter has been accused of being involved in cases jointly with the refugee chief of trying to delude or misinform Mr. Whilden as to the state of the refugees. Mr. Whilden's office is in the same building with Mr. Husick's.

7 A Garden Becomes a Moon

Think of hot mercury trickling out
or molten silver pouring in a dish.
The webs and sluggish river loops
winked up the sun's burst blooms
as the plane droned home to Saigon.
Zipped in a green vinyl sack
shutting the stinks together, the body
shook on the rivet-rattling floor.
Strapped in, the two friends sat
staring at each other's shoes, the sack,
their hands, the banana-green sack. The pilot
sipped warm Coke and radioed the morgue.
In the cratered Strike Zone far below
smoke drifted up from a fragmented tomb.
A man burnt incense at his father's grave.

Before their clouding, before closing, one sees
oneself in the eyes of the dead,
eyes of the children cut down like skinny chickens,
eyes of the small-breasted women, wiry men.
Those who became completely wise cried out
as the slugs shattered the windshield,
glass flying into spider webs,
as skipping bullets slivered their eyes.
Gitelson, do-gooder? a fool?
Am I a Christer and your corpse-monger?
Dead, I am your father, brother. Dead, we are your son.

For Mary Bui Thi Khuy, 1944–1969

Dear Christ, I pray for Mary Khuy
whose youth and pleasant purity,
smile and easy ways,
remind me, in the bitter days,
that Grace is heaven's surety
for goodness, earth's repay.

Let Grace that is in women blessed,
ease us now. And at the hour of our death.

The Dragonfish

Brown men shock the brown pools with nets.
Fishing for mudfish, carp and *ca loc,*
they step and stalk the banks; hurl;
stand, then squat heronlike in the
shadow-stretching, red evening dusk.

The pond is lovely where they fish,
one of many in a marshy field
linking delta paddies about Cao Lanh.
Phenol streaks, chartreuse and smoke blue,
curl, clot and twirl over the manila-bright,
sun-slanting surface, while silver chubs
flash after garbage scraps chugging out,
churning up, from an opening drain.

Five old tombs shadow the pond's far edge.
Their dripping stones are cut in characters
which no one, now, can read. Ghosts
of landlords click their tallies there.
Rain roils the water. Ducks dally
through twining blue morning-glory
trellising in spirals
over concertina barbed wire.
Like swallows or a weaver's shuttles,
darting jets, F-105s,
ply the curling fringes of the storm.
Rain spatters—wind scatters—
the water turned gun-barrel blue.
In sheeting rain, a wet dog grins
from a worn tomb's washing steps.
The dog snuffles a hen's feather.
It crackles old bones.

Far out in deserted paddies
more cratered than the moon,
guerrillas of the Front hide themselves
beneath slabs of rain-eaten tombs:
patient are they as lampwicks.

In squalling waters, North and South,
fishermen dredge, draw, dragnet up
a heavy fish, a dragon fish,
a land in the shape of the dragonfish.

To P.T., a Poet, Who Holds That Good Poets Are Always Nice People (Even Robert Frost)

If I have descended like the locust,
wings filmy, bright, whirring ambitions,
with mandible greed for green expanses,
for tended lushest leaf, all foliage,
surely the wing-beats of survival are,
while desperate, familiar to a poet's ear.
Think of deserts you've devoured clean.
Poets are *not* nice people, though locusts sing.

Epithalamium for Alex Clokie Clarke

Seeking necessity, she only found
a dotty Englishman, drunk on the ground.
Up helping him gently, by the balls,
he made a pass—gently—at her wherewithals.
Married at morning, no one gave bail.
He wore black pajamas; she, a flypaper veil.
Now practice they arts, forward and black.
He calls her his Filly; she calls him her Snack.
May Mary uphold them and good Jesus Christ.
May Britain forgive them their Orient vice.

Bereft of Morpheus, a Poet Is Visited by His Muse

Virtuoso of the short line,
of epigrammatic sequence,
abed the poet stretched him out
and pondered human weakness.

At times he squeezed a pimple
along his ropy penis
or spread a scrotal wrinkle
with fingers not the cleanest.

Greeted by a milky ribbon,
draining out in lazy ooze,
he turned his thoughts to women
and invoked his curious Muse.

Composing quickly, writing fast,
he found his central theme:
of love amid these hardened times,
of female stealth and schemes.

Sorely lamenting the plight of men
who, sensitive and true,
found it most impossible
to find someone to screw,

he turned his face unto the wall,
turned off the bedside lamp,
and yawned, then scratched his
pubic hair, quite sticky now and damp.

The Field

Under the snow-packed, snow-snapped hemlocks,
beneath the withering rhododendron,
the black creek churns out.
Plodding by in yellow boots,
I enjoy the snowfall's invigoration
as Hitler must have, snow-
tramping to the teahouse at Obersalzberg.
Snow crunching; boot tags jingle
and a farm dog yammers in the valley's
dusk snow-sheen. Squinting north, I see
the snow-in-the-twig–shrouded mountains.
A fist of oak leaves stirs. Blue smoke
puffs out my cabin's chimney.
The logs are snapping in an empty room.
I am creek-wise of unwilled purpose;
mountain-taught of possibility.
If I say this to lover or to friend,
will they walk with my words in the snow?

Venturing Out

Translation of a Vietnamese folk lyric

Each evening, ducks paddle, egrets fly;
Mr. Elephant snaps sugar cane then strides into the jungle.
I'll follow there to strip rattan plaits,
fetching them home to make a sling for you to go peddling.
Selling at no loss: why, that's profit.
Go on, have a look at the Sun's face, at the Moon's.

Harvesting Ducks

The one, with dark and meditative eye,
dappled head and yellow pebbled legs,
saw the blade letting at its gorge
and blinked asleep, blood spattering dry leaves.
The other thrashed its heavy cornstalk wings:
tangled them oddly about the snaking neck, the cut
windpipe sumping blood and crackling air.
And soon, bellies slit and emptied, trussed,
plucked, scaly feet strung from a branch,
someone saw the horror of making a poem
of sifting, downy feathers and inches of gut.

Talking About Birds

Translation of a Vietnamese folk lyric

Listen. Listen here, all about birds and beasts:
Sexy and alluring? That's the little Moorhen.
Manner offends? That's nasty Cormorant.
Slave like an ant, that's the traveling Teal.
Straining to overhear? Drongos snoop in trees.
Shaky in its knees, the skinny, brown Egret.
Stays at home each night, that's cowardly Snipe.
Hungry for their tripe, the Pelicans carouse.
Hungry by the house; there, the darting Larks.
Pole the shallow bark; Peacock plies his art.
Red crest, blue feathers, that's a jungle Pheasant.
Bickering unpleasant? That's the sneaky Plover
Got a magic Book of Colors: the Soothsayer Hawk.
Never married, never caught, that's Wanderer Grebe.
Mate long since dead: the poor Widow-Wed.
Heart as thick as lead, that's the teasing Jay.
Eggs, but won't lay? Duckbirds live that way.

Sitting around, talking about kinds of birds,
Offspring grow up and look for each other.
See, the Weaver is clever and wise.
The Owl nests only at the edge of the island.
Watch: the Magpies have brought some news;
If they hover then call, our sisters are coming.
The Crows, now, are really just like us, cawing
From far off, "Wash up. The journey's over."

Riddle: The Heart, like a Calf's Head, When?

When the spindly calf sprawls by the barn,
frozen a week in the hay-manure ice. When
a cockle-burred stray and the starved barn cats
have gnawed the heart's eye to the white
socket bone, and severed hems of nerves flutter.
Here: the dog skulks back; his chin-fur crimsoned,
he tunnels in the heart's cracked cage, lapping
a soup of liver and lung, sours his gut, pukes
suet-mess in tractor rut, then snouts in for more.
When the heart is two-headed. Over-large. Without tooth.

A Grain of Actuality Begins the Poem

The sunshine streamed the rain-pocked sand
and glared off keening gulls
that squabbled over shellfish meats.

In tidal pools the pipers waded
on twig-legs, stabbing for starfish
with scissored, poking, needle bills.

Beetles scurried dry sea weeds.
The air heaved with a heavy smell.
Even the sun was hungry.

About the brilliant beach was scattered
a seaweed-strung and rotting wrack-heap
of mussel shells with grinning gums.

Nicely like a pearl is a poem
begun with an accidental speck
from the ocean of the actual.

A grain, a grit, which once admitted
irritates the mantle of thought
and coats itself in lacquers of the mind.

For Miss Tin in Hue

The girl (captured; later, freed)
and I (cut by a centimeter of lead)
remember well the tea you steeped
for us in the garden, as music played
and the moon plied the harvest dusk.
You read the poem on a Chinese vase
that stood outside your father's room,
where he dozed in a mandarin dream
of King Gia Long's reposing at Ben Ngu.
We worry that you all are safe.
A house with pillars carved in poems
is floored with green rice fields;
and roofed by all the heavens of this world.

Country Excursion: A Brown Study Collage

cigarette-butt stain on the toilet bowl's lip.
maple-seed cockroach wing on the family altar.
a pork chop flung high over the stucco cemetery wall:
to the dozen or so lepers dwelling inside.
acres of tassled rice like Kansas harvest wheat.
dark robes of monks in an open boat, cutting a furrow
on the silted river.
a convoy of artillery pieces caked in mud.
a water buffalo stretched in a mud wallow; dead, its
huge side gouged crimson by .50-millimeter slugs.
miles of mud greasing the roadway to Saigon.
sipping root beer from a straw in a clear, plastic bag.

Rain

"A mosaic of a man . . . like a mosaic of the weather."
—Wallace Stevens, letter to S. M. B. Quinn

The straight rain drops
through the last red leaves
in the black branches
of the crab apple, spills
quickly down the slopes,
leaching the earth clean
of track, of footprint.
Sparrows scurry like fleas
through the dripping skein
of the stone wall's dead ivy.
The raindrops, collecting
in the bearded branches
of a hemlock, fall
one by one.

Like an old woman
this field lies
on her sickbed,
washed and washed
by these windless
winter rains.
From her scrawny flesh
no smell rises.
Her scalp is pink clean
under thin willow hair.
The bush is worn down
to weak wood. Say
that her nails are pared.
She is left to sleep awhile.

A stump green as copper
at the bottom of the sea,
covered with mosses
and polyps
with bright red nodes.

Dropped into the snow,
seeds wriggle blindly
to put their heat.
Lichen and little plants
creep forth as fast
as the snow recedes.

Riddlingly, the rain
cuts the snow until
the melt-run's quick tongue
rills lightly over the roof
of the brook's icy mouth.
This field will melt to mud;
this muddy sea will bud
clumps of grass, clots
of green amid stubbled husks,
floating like emerald kelp
across the flat thawing fields.

Look. Bees are risking the cold
blooms of the March rain,
swimming in the sidewalk daffodils.
Filthily, the gutters run high.
Last night, geese flew over
honking hysterically
like saxophones with split reeds.
When they passed we heard again
the sound of tires
cutting the flooded streets:
a sound of ripping bedsheets.

After the rain, the light broke
on a herd darkly dotting
a hillside pasture: glistening
and washed with sunlight.

Steam smokes up from cowflaps
under the sheltering elms.
Gnats on diaphanous wings
are treading the sun-shafted air.
Sage and thistle and butterflyweed
sparkle and wink and drip.

Nixon Imperator Augustus

When Claudius weighed the edict
giving his divine consent
to farting at the banquet table
years of conquest had fallen
since Cornelia's aristocratic jewels,
Tiberius and Gaius Gracchus,
misfortuned the Republic
with vague notions of equity
only to win for themselves
popularity and assassination.
A law to fart by is, surely,
as much a sign of the times
as Nero's nightly garden parties
lit by pitch-dipped Christians.
On the subject Suetonius says little,
but, no doubt, certain patricians squawked
(as Rome met Parthian, Dacian, and Pict)
that the barbarian defeats had derived
from turning the Field of Mars
into a park of statuary; while others,
less loudly, griped about Cato's
fabulous and ill-gotten wealth.
But who can forget Tiberius?
the emperor dubbed "Callipedes"
in memory of that favorite mime
who played the long-distance runner
without ever treading a step.

A Riddle

Winde ic on windbland   wīde ofer eorþan
On foldwege forð   ond folcsteðe.
Ofer dēop wæter   mid dugoðe ic drīfe;
Mid sǣlīðend slǣpe   on swanrāde.
Monn sēcan mot   micle twǣm ēagum,
Nǣfre mæg hē   mec ǣfre sēon.
Gif ic gielpe,   gylpwordum sprǣce,
Scamode beoð scēotend   ic scende hira mōd.
Wast hwæt þu nū   ic wurde nemde?
Wæs mīn ealdfaeder Aldhelm,   ǣnlic manna,
Wæs Malmesburh mīn mōder,   Maildubhes mynster.
Rǣd þu mec: ᚱ   Ic ride snūde
To hāme mid hæleð.   Hāt mec swā: ᚠ
Ond, nū ic bringe nīed,   swā nemne mec: ᚷ
Hoga, hæleð.   Saga hwæt ic hātte.

I ride on the wind gust   wide over the earth
across the earthways   and over farm folk.
Over deep water   I drive with men.
With sailors I sleep   on the swan road.
A man could search a lot   with his two eyes
but never would he   ever see me.
If I boast,   if I speak boast words,
embarrassed are the archers   for I shame them.
Now do you know   what I am called?
Aldhelm was my grandfather   best of men.
Malmesbury was my mother   Maildubhe's monastery.
You can read me *R*ad   for quickly I ride
home with the warriors.   Also call me *U*r.
And, since I bring trouble,   call me *N*eed.
Think, man.   Say what I am called.

The answer to the riddle is: Riddle.

A Latter-Day Saxon Bathes at Bournemouth

"Swā sāe bebūgeth
windegeard, weallas."
—*Beowulf,* 1224

Echoing sly chicaneries
canary-birds of false note,
bright startles trope my tongue
with sighs and lies and little gloats
when the wind skims the sea,
that green windyard.

An ugly squeal-full is my lilt
when tides rake the shore
and shell scoops rattle
and skipping wrinkles run the bore
when winds scrape the sea,
that fierce windyard.

Oh, my pink little piggies
will pat the beach.
Palms up, I'll dance
where grunions screech.
I'll willy-nilly wheel
and keen like a gull,

when the wind whines
and rides the pines
blows up billows
and seaweed balls
and smacks in hard
from a bleak windyard.

Palindrome for Clyde Coreil in Saigon

Pigeons flutter in the eaves of the Music Bldg;
here there are a number of beautiful women.
Amid the clutter of books on my desk,
I prop my feet, lean back, and read.
Hot lunches are served at a cafeteria nearby.
Each afternoon, I pick up *The Times*.
A secretary brews coffee. I get paid for talking
to students who don't care what I say
about subjects I don't care to talk about.
When I can afford them, I buy good cigars.

Every now and then, you get cigars from home.
Puffing on one, you dicker with a shopgirl
over the price of a breakfast of frenchbread
and black coffee in a sugar-bottomed glass.
You study newsprint on a wrapper of dried squid.
Elephant grass and rice fields expand beyond the city.
Returning at evening, your feet plod along a street
crunching with fishheads, roaches, and shattered glass.
A bargirl telephones to see if you'll be in. Outside,
music flutters in the wings of rising pigeons.

Letter from a Bargirl

(found in a typewriter)

```
                my dearest darling
          hi/  how are you
      ihop eeveything is abight with you,iam fine
im imi    i miss you verym  m uch
      doy yovm/  you miss me/
                fuck you
          iwant to fuck youp


      i think about you all time
       you alays in myha heart

    makæ love na
              make . love . not.. war ........

  fuck....you


                Monique
```

Communiqué

(found tacked to a door)

Kien Phong Province chief respectfully inform to the people the following:

Since the need for special security, I declare the

curfew in Kien Phong province from 10 pm to 5 a. m that takes effect from the issued date to issuing new order.

Please, all the people, abide by this curfuw to avoid danger and disturbance from the security agencies.

In emergency case, the passengers should use light and

have I D card whenever security agents want to check.

CAO LANH, August 16th 1967

Province chief, Kien Phong.

L T. Col. Doan van Guong

Li Po and the Peacock King

When the court poet, Li Po,
was in his summer years
he was fond of watching
the river's autumn mists
rise up and drift away,
leaving the bank's willows
bare and cleanly naked.

During the autumn rains
he dwelt under bamboo thatch
listening to the furious tatter:
He pictured his pavilion
a resounding drum.
The poet Li Po said he tried
for many hours to describe
the rain's intended rhythm.
He found the effort, vain;
the enterprise, absurd.

When older he complained
to find the winter willows
bare and wretched; the river,
fetid; the pines, spidery;
the air, dank; the hills, inane.
In his thoughts, he said,
he heard the peacock screech.
Its cry, he said,
could slit the thread
even of the strongest sensibility.

"Work the Untrammeled Style,"
said an I-p'in painter whom Li sought.
"Seek the Undeliberate," advised
a Ch'an master. Li smiled.

When it rained he heard only
the slap of the courtesans' feet
dancing before the Emperor,
or nothing at all,
or the shriek of the peacock.
"Kung-Chiao Ming-Wang.

O Peacock King," he cried,
"Devourer of evil thoughts,
of sickly passions,
fix tightly your talons
in my shoulders' flesh.
Shred my mind clean. Spread
the fan of your bright plumage
in my thoughts like a thousand eyes."
But the Bird King was away,
flying in summer marshes.

When the sage Li Po
was in his winter years
he left court and retired
and became a silent man
journeying up the River Kiang.
Although he called Him many times,
the Peacock King was always with him.

Sunset Along the Shore

As the wind might tightly wrap
a loose sail about a spar,

these yellow clouds collect
in curls across the pelvic sky

about the sun as it slips
into the licking sea

like some blonde bather
walking slowly into warm waves

which swell above her limbs
to swallow the sun and sweep to shore.

At the Exiled King's River Pavilion

Translation of a Vietnamese folk lyric

Evening. Before the King's pavilion:
people are sitting, some fish, some are sad and grieving,
some loving, in love, remembering, waiting, watching.
Whose boat plies the river mists,
offering so many rowing songs
that move these Mountains and Rivers, our Nation?

Polluted Place

I would not stick my hand in it,
the polluted river
with its scaly stones—stones
like dirty fruit with peeling skins.

My God, the fish bobbed about,
milky bellies up,
like bottles with shredding labels.
No boat would set out.

A heron swooped over it
low and darkly
like a scowl, but would not land.
Oil slicked the surface of the ooze.

The trees crept away from its banks.

Don Diego Garcia

Died, 1286. Sarcophagus in Fogg Museum, Cambridge, Massachusetts

Your pillow, Don Diego,
The wooden pillow of your sarcophagus,
Don Diego Garcia,
Has split beneath
The centuries-weight of your head.
Woodworms, my lord,
Riddle your effigy;
Eat at your knightly robes.
Yet, at your feet
Lies crushed forever
The Animal Vice.
The peace of your Lord in Heaven
Abides you yet, Don Diego, while
The weight of our lives presses hard.
Whatever man you may have been,
Don Diego Garcia,
A woodcutter has saved you.

Ship of Redemption

Translation of a Vietnamese Folk lyric

The bell of Linh Mu Pagoda tolls,
awakening the drowsy soul,
probing, reminding one of debt,
washing one clean of worldly dust.
A boat crosses to the Western Lands.

A Court Is Likened to an Inner Landscape

Standing anyplace in this square,
each elm has its certain distance.
Wandering beneath the elms,
one sees a constant shifting.
At times the leaves are green
as copper at the bottom of the sea;
sometimes, as brown as kelp iodine.

These elms, in their distancing,
shades of green, and casts of shadow,
are moments in the mind: definite
or indefinite as sunshine. Memories
drift gull-like through the rose evening.
A shiver of light on low branches
holds a vision of April days.
Overhead, strange birds wheel and glide.

To one standing here at evening,
their arabesques are curious
and remote as clouds on a seaside day.
"Augur them as I may," he says,
"they have little to do with me.
The court has four perimeters
through which none enters or leaves."

For him, as he watches the evenings,
hopes blow like gusted leaves.
His lips are shut like evening clover.

On a Photograph of Schoolchildren Wearing Gas Masks. Rheims. World War I.

In 1916
these twenty-some children stood
as prepared as they could
wrapped in makeshift masks
to choke back the lung-eating gas.

By 1940,
if any were still alive
and guilty of such human crimes
as love, marriage, children, friends,
they doubled the dead in the streets of Rheims.

On August 6, 1945
in Rheims on a summer day after the war
did there appear stigmata like sores
and birth stains, as Japanese
children popped like burning rubber trees?

In 1954
the French dug at Dien Bien Phu
a grave in a valley. A fish grew
into a dragon dancing in blood,
staining jungle and delta mud.

April, 1965:
Passing over gutted villages
our bombers drop our Commander's message:
"If gas again is in the air,
our conscience, and lungs, are clear."

Children at Play and at Sleep

Why did the schoolboys look in the ditch?
I looked to see the minnows itch
and dart and wiggle in the reeking pool.

What fishy sperm and ithic egg
kissed in the midst of drain-ditch plague?
Wondrous where cold creatures dwell.

I looked and saw in the sewage drain
the face of a child on a magazine:
lifting, shredding, wadding apart.

The children looked into the sky
at a copter skipping like a dragonfly.
I visioned an infant in amber light;

then saw an angel, ugly, wild,
rat-hairy, snatch the infant child
and dunk him deep headfirst in filth.

The babe sucked ooze with ruptured lungs;
then wriggled fat feet and gagged on his tongue.
He swelled with heat; became a bug.

At nights I walk Can Tho's poor streets
and sneak by mats where children sleep
wrapped larvalike in gauzy cotton nets.

71

The House at Evening

The rats danced on the loud tin roof;
slipped and tumbled, slip-slapping their tails;
scratched their nails, clattered and clawed.
A black big bug dropped off the wall.
Plop on its back. To wriggle legs
ever so evilly, nastily alive.
In an ugly winkling, little things
felt; hurried, scurried, crawled
on quick and too many hairy legs.
By moonlight and a chorus of peepers
a toad leaped in the grass outside,
until a yellow beam of light
locked a signal in its eye.
From bough to bough a spider spread its nets.

Some Commonplaces of the Times

If Sister Isabella Victorina
were sent to have her uterus scraped
it need not draw wiseacre japes
concerning immaculate conception.

The New York City Dept. of Health holds
that "VD is no camp." Indeed, traces
are often found floating in public places
—urethral wreaths, smokily alive.

It is a plausible event, not odd,
when unwed mother makes a fourth-story leap
to crush unborn child and herself to sleep.
A man's brain has a sorry root.

No more strange, nor humorous,
than the musky, sexual scent of blossoms
of the hawthorn are these our sins,
our fears of breeding which we are bred to.

May Letter

When we strayed last by the river
it shone dully
alloyed with a pewter sky.

The season was when cherry
and plum trees
stretched tightly their white blossoms.

Now their flowers melt like snow
on the lush leaves.
The turtle hisses under a May Apple.

A cardinal dances above daisies
claiming a field.
The mockingbird squats in the bare mimosa.

Four kinds of lilac choke my window vase,
each fading in turn.
Four shades from white to deep purple.

Soon to your window will come the oriole
and the finch.
If one drops a feather, make a wish.

Hand-Painted Birthday Card:
Abandoned Farmhouse

Even in spring's sun-dried season
the daffodils toss in the yard,
choking the splintered doorsill
of the house overcome by collapse.
Each year the bulbs root further
filling the clearing floor goldenly
with trembling cups, low to the grass.
Bagworms, with sticky-coned cocoons,
needle by needle swallow a spruce
whose branches shake unpleasantly
with each wormbug's ugly wriggle.
See, too, the heap of molding feathers
under the belled forsythia:
A catbird's breast once hatched song;
now mothering snaky vermin.
But simple rains water equally
the accidental beauties, the incidental
horrors. On this day, your birthday,
I wish you ease of impulse and
a sense of what you own already:
the loveliness to bear it to beauty.

Peleus Sees the Birth of Aphrodite

Her thin face half-turned, I found her standing naked as the water at her feet: languid, brown, smooth. The glare of calm shallows caught at her blonde hair and held her by the ankles where she stood, captive, weight on one full hip, cupping a breast in one hand. (Wife, forgive me, the memory of her back's curve, those apple breasts and slim thighs make tongue and hands ache with telling.) The Sun and Sea licked joyfully at their new daughter. The Winds played with her hair.

That she was a goddess and surely evil, I could tell. I could tell by the knot of fish, black and glebous, that swirled, stretched, curled and recoiled in the waves rocking at her feet. The way the girl looked when I shouted! Slowly turning her head, slowly lifting her eyes, slowly smiling. Love, the tremble in the cup you offer betrays your fear. What harm can she cause? Why, yesterday I saw her with her same-boned mother who was gross, loose-fleshed, and not nearly so pleasing as you, Thetis.

Lines from the Arabic

How many times in bitter rage
did I think of you with your family,
fearful lest they be kind?
Once, in February, I saw a photograph
of your opening gifts at Christmas.
I worried a week while snows melted,
believing love so easily lost.

Now I hunch elbows to knees
in a rattan chair, in a tropic land
years away. The sun bites my neck
as I turn a book of poems
which you gave me, years ago.
I find in it a yellowed marker
where you had been reading Shelley's
"Lines From the Arabic," which run
that, despite suns and seas,
two lovers' hearts are always one.

In Hyperborea

It is, Odysseus, as if you had drowned
on leaving Circe's isle, or sank below
sucking Charybdis, for northern gusts
bite your eyes like fish in turgid seas.
With pointed cap askew and frosting breath,
a whitened beard, you bear the well-made oar.
Among strange peoples once again, devout
of prophecy, you seek the journey's end.
Dead Tiresias promised death at sea.
Midwinter. Small birds cry sharply, pecking out
the sun from rocks and vines. Day's lord
glooms out: a poor bloodless bantam preens
his skinny feathers by a wattled oaken door.
A pungent heat, of fodder, straw, manure,
tossed on the snow this morning, steams the air,
while barn-held horses stamp and chew. Odysseus,
plodding by, weeps for dead Penelope,
for King Telemachus, irresolute of mind.
He calls Athena, but the wily man
already knows: in snow-enshrouding lands
Athena is a stunted owl in smoke beblackened rafters.

Midnight at Phoenix Island in the Mekong

Flat-footed, squatting on the rickety jakes
catwalked on stilts plunged into the current
and shaken by tidal slosh and misty gusts.
In the next stall a tubercular monk hacks and spits
into moonshoals swallowing every human token:
Roman coin, Thai celadon, sundered Cham navies,
black opium bricks, tribute girls chokered in gold,
French bibles and cannon, spittle and shit.
A nighthawk bleats and skims the inky trees.
A hazy moon, scavenged by apes prying up rocks
that may yet mirror a human face, spans out
across the river in a funnel of rickling troughs.

In Pittsburgh apartments, the moon traces
crackled veneers on Victorian dressers, probes
snaking hair cracks on smooth washbowls, glints
off the dead T.V. A baby rattle gleams

Moon-struck, a gunboat drifts anchor.
More harrowing than its barrels' random barks
is the screak of an office chair pulled out from a desk.
At dawn the milk-eyed dead evoke the thorough belief
that bullets pierce only flesh, usually just once.

Saying Good-by to Mr. and Mrs. My,
Saigon, 1972

"The ancients liked to write about natural beauty."
—Ho Chi Minh, "Cam Tuong Doc *Thien Gia Thi*"

In earlier times poets brushed on printed silk
those poems about clouds, mountains, and love.
Nowadays, when "poems are cased in steel," poets know
that literary words only limit and lie,
that fine words only tug at the ear.
A poet had better keep his mouth shut, we say,
unless he's found words to comfort and teach.
Today, comfort and teaching themselves deceive
and it takes cruelty to make any friends
when it is a lie to speak, a lie to keep silent.
Wise to this, most men talk too much. A few
trail morning beaches studying seadrift, marveling
at curls broken bare in crushed shells,
at the sheen and cracks of laved, salted wood,
at the pearling blues of rock-stuck mussels,
each odd as friends: accidental; fragmented.

Erhart

"Birds have nests; men have ancestors."
—*Vietnamese proverb*

1   Standing in a soybean field,
on a rocky scarp above the sea,
the two of us, in dispossessed thirties,
scan nude bathers on the shore below,
as gulls, winged flesh all salt,
might scour for shellfish.
Angry and red on Erhart's belly
the football stitch stings with sweat
where they cut into his cancer.
But look at him here today:
climbing cliffs, getting his peek,
dismayed only that the naked man below
who sidles into a tide-cut cave
lures not a girl, but another gay.
As I watch him watch a girl in the surf,
Erhart remarks that "birds have nests;
foxes have their holes, but the Son of Man
hath nowhere to lay his head."
"Birds have nests," I add. "Men have ancestors."
Erhart's father died manic and alone.
A whore-child gave birth to Erhart
at 27, in Asia, across the Pacific
that glints on these bathers and defies our stare.

2 Outside Middlesex hospital
the student unions queue,
marching behind a rent-all truck
from which a band plays "Hello, Dolly."
They want bigger scholarships.
Inside Middlesex, a blonde moppet
zaps Erhart with cobalts
to make his cancer go away,
those narsty modes, that ugly clavicle
blossoming into a Kali-flower.
She says it will be all right:
Never once has she died
for all the patients she's radiated.
Erhart is going to India to meet
a wonderful Indian guru, leaving England
to its henna-haired boys and big women.
Outside, the Bobbies badger the crowd.
Inside Erhart's insides
his ionized cells are blue with rage
like Tantric demons blue-faced with rage.

3   At night, by the Ganges, by a pyre guttering
    foul smoke and gaseous licks of flame,
    by a dog gnawing the ankle and foot
    of a woman cremated during the day,
    Erhart, hunched as if he had a chest cold,
    pisses on a flat rock and looks up at stars,
    at Berenice's Hair, at the Lost Pleiades,
    at Orion about to hurl his spear of stars.
    In L.A., a G.P. thought Erhart had an ulcer.
    The surgery didn't work. After the vegetable
    diet, the German carrot-juice treatment,
    the yoga chants, the asanas, the "breaths of fire,"
    after the sautéed-lemon-rind cure,
    the acupuncturist, the Reichian masseuse,
    after all the death-defying fucking in London,
    Erhart has come to see Sai Baba
    who can materialize Swiss watches
    and pillars of holy ash. (But can he kill the Big C?)
    What else is left? Filipino psychic surgeons?
    If one plays at dying, he doesn't die at all.
    (In a closet in my farmhouse in Pennsylvania
    Erhart's manuscripts fill his flight bag,
    stories and articles, published and unpublished,
    the film clips he shot on battlefields in Vietnam).

The river tide washes the embers of the dead.
Erhart, diving and flying in a whirl of methadone
and realization, watches for star-nesting birds;
spies a man-bird: beaked, crimson-winged,
with a body of gold—Garuda,
who routed the gods, their wheel of blades,
who severed the snake guard, spat back its poison,
whose wing-beat rush could stop the world.
Who spat back the poison. Who dwells in the sun.

Keep moving, friend, and don't look down.

PITT POETRY SERIES